Agnes Jones

Felicity McCall

GUILDHALL PRESS

First published in October 2006

Guildhall Press
Unit 15
Ráth Mór Business Park
Bligh's Lane
Derry BT48 0LZ
T: (028) 7136 4413 F: (028) 7137 2949
info@ghpress.com www.ghpress.com

Cover design and illustrations: Joe Campbell

Produced in association with Greater Shantallow Community Arts
ISBN 0 946451 96 6
ISBN 978 0 946451 96 8

We gratefully acknowledge the financial support of both Derry City Council and Donegal County Council.

COMHAIRLE CHONTAE
Dhun na nGall
DONEGAL COUNTY COUNCIL

DERRY CITY COUNCIL

Contents

Acknowledgements

The author wishes to thank Mike Kelly and David Charters (Liverpool), and Mary J Devlin and Margaret McGrath (Donegal) for their help in her research; Oliver Green, Joe Campbell and all at Greater Shantallow Community Arts for their hard work, support and creativity; Paola Bernardelli and Ambient Light Productions for the use of images; Peter Jones and family, New Zealand, for providing a unique letter of tribute to Agnes from Florence Nightingale, which rounded off the story so well; Guildhall Press for their professional input; and Derry City Council and Donegal County Council for their commitment to ensuring the Agnes Jones project is only beginning.

Preface

When I first discovered Agnes Jones's overgrown grave hidden away in the old St Mura's Church of Ireland graveyard in Fahan, I had no idea where my journey to find out more about Ireland's nursing pioneer would take me. Nor could I imagine the inspirational story I would piece together from archive material, contemporary letters, extracts from her own diaries, the painstaking research of others and out-of-print publications which I tracked down. This material enabled me to write and produce the original stage play with valuable insights into Agnes's life and work.

The reasons this pioneering woman remains largely forgotten at home are myriad. First, there's her family's desire that there should be no great memorial erected to her at the time of her death; coupled with the fact that, with Agnes's generation gone, the Joneses effectively died out in the Fahan area. As a military family, they would never have fully integrated with the indigenous farming and fishing community; they may also have been set apart by their religion (Church of Ireland), though there is no doubt that Agnes's ministry was a cross-community one. And while she was a devout leader of prayers and bible reading, she takes pains to point out in her diaries that anyone from another tradition who took part did so *'entirely at their own volition'*. Hers was never a mission to convert.

Although she was one of Florence Nightingale's first twelve trainee nurses at St Thomas's Hospital in London, there are suggestions that there were personality differences between the two women, and it was only in the declining years of her long life that Miss Nightingale accorded Agnes Jones the accolades she so richly deserves – and, even then, often referring to her by the pseudonym Agnes's sister Josephine also used for her, Una. Any specific reasons for the choice of name are lost.

Myths and misconceptions abound, as they tend to do with historically significant figures. I was regularly assured by (well-intentioned) amateur historians that Agnes Jones had nursed in the Crimea, that her father was the rector in Fahan and that she is buried in her adopted city of Liverpool. In fact, although she had travelled extensively across Europe and had studied in Germany, her entire nursing career was spent in England, largely among the expatriate Irish. Her cortège leaving Brownlow Hill workhouse was one of the largest Liverpool had ever seen, but her remains were taken home to her beloved Fahan where she lay, largely forgotten, for more than a century in the overgrown St Mura's graveyard. Only at the instigation of determined well-wishers was a signpost erected on the main Derry to Buncrana road indicating the location of the graveyard.

The breakthrough in my research came through contact with two Liverpool writers, historian Mike Kelly and journalist David Charters. For them, and for the Liverpool Irish community, Agnes remains a legend. She is remembered in the Anglican and Catholic traditions, in the medical services and the department of Liverpool-Irish studies at the University of Liverpool. An awe-inspiring Italian marble statue to her stands in the city's oratory. If Florence Nightingale is remembered as *The Lady with the Lamp*, then, for the people of Liverpool, Agnes Jones is *The Lady in the Staircase Window* in the city's Anglican cathedral.

Mike Kelly and David Charters's support for, and faith in, our project has been as generous as it has been unwavering.

After the stage play of *Agnes* was performed by Handful Productions at Derry's Playhouse in November and December 2004, directed by Bernie Mahon, it was decided to write a screenplay based on my research.

The project was adopted by Greater Shantallow Community Arts and developed further with the involvement of the Derry-based film production company, Ambient Light.

The short documentary-drama *Agnes* was filmed in the summer of 2006 using professional and community-based resources, with Derry's Bronagh Gallagher in the title role. After the première at the Foyle Film Festival, it will tour the festival circuit as well as being screened on television.

This illustrated book has been produced to coincide with the première and to support the cross-border, cross-community campaign for a permanent and fitting memorial to Agnes Jones in the North West.

Felicity McCall

A Memorial to Agnes

Research for the script and planning for the film inevitably took the production team to Liverpool, where Agnes Jones was matron of the workhouse from 1865–68. Her memory is revered by both traditions there and nowhere more so than among the medical profession and the Irish community. The Anglican cathedral has a stained-glass window commemorating her, and there is a marble statue of her as an angel of mercy in the oratory. Yet her grave in Fahan, where she grew up, was unmarked until recently. The only other memorials to this remarkable woman in the area are a plaque in St Mura's Church of Ireland church in Fahan and the official name of the former nurses' home at Altnagelvin Hospital in Derry.

By buying this book, you have endorsed the campaign to have a fitting, permanent memorial erected to Agnes Jones in the part of Ireland she called home. A percentage from each book sold will go towards a fund to develop this memorial, which will be tangible evidence that the people of the North West are proud of this woman of achievement. Her vision, tireless determination, cross-community ethos and sheer humanity remain as inspirational today as they were a century and a half ago.

Foreword by Oliver Green

Although I spent many happy childhood times in the area around Fahan in County Donegal, where we had relatives, I confess to having known little about Agnes Jones until I became involved with Felicity McCall's research for a stage play based on her life and work. I immediately realised that here was an unsung heroine whose work crossed all boundaries of faith, class or nationality, and who deserved greater recognition in our social history.

As we began turning the research into a screenplay, the idea gathered momentum until a modest community arts project became a full partnership between the community and private sectors. Derry-based film company Ambient Light joined the production team and we set about making a definitive documentary drama, entitled, simply, *Agnes.*

Agnes's story has captured the public imagination in an inspirational way which enabled us to cast such luminaries of the acting world as Bronagh Gallagher, in the title role, and Dan Gordon as our narrator. The wealth of talent which is active in the Greater Shantallow area was given full expression in everything from composing and recording the original soundtrack and title song – an unforgettable, haunting performance from Betty Joyce, which captures the mood perfectly – to the authentic costumes created with meticulous attention to detail by the Galliagh Women's Group. This irrepressible group also kept us well fed on location and, on occasion, doubled as film extras, joining the dozens of enthusiastic amateurs from across Ireland and beyond who gave of their best.

As the dream became reality, locations were made available, and Ulster Television expressed an interest in broadcasting the finished documentary drama. Finally came the news that the Northern Ireland Film and Television Commission had approved grant funding. Local investment quickly followed. So did enquiries about screening *Agnes*. Others asked was there a book available? Now, thanks to the enterprise, skill and commitment of Derry publishing company Guildhall Press, there is.

We believe this publication will help to establish this remarkable woman's rightful place in history, and will share a flavour of the remarkable journey we have undertaken – and are still travelling.

Our thanks to the Mayor, Helen Quigley, and Derry City Council, for generously enabling us to create a little piece of history in such lavish style – and playing their part in ensuring that one of our most remarkable daughters will not be forgotten.

Oliver Green
General Manager, Greater Shantallow Community Arts
Co-Producer, *Agnes*

Foreword by the Mayor of Derry

As Mayor of Derry, I am delighted to host the official launch of the Agnes Jones Project. I am confident that this excellent documentary-drama and accompanying book will establish forever the vital role played by this visionary nursing pioneer.

Agnes Jones grew up in the North West and, regardless of where her vocation took her, continued to regard it as her spiritual home and chose it for her final resting place.

We should be proud of her and accord her the place in history she so richly deserves.

Although she lived and worked more than 150 years ago, Nurse Jones's determination to pursue her life's ambition in the face of bureaucratic intransigence, social convention, ill-founded family concerns and, often, poor health, is still a valid role model for women today.

Discrimination, sexism and anti-Irish feeling were but minor obstacles in Agnes Jones's tireless campaign for the welfare of the workhouse inmates, and to be a voice for those she called the *'poorest of the poor'*, regardless of creed, race or nationality.

As well as a tribute to a remarkable woman, I see this project as the beginning of a life revisited, so that its achievements and message can be recognised across her beloved North West, Agnes's adopted city of Liverpool, and beyond.

Mayor Helen Quigley
Derry City Council

Foreword by the County Mayor of Donegal

On behalf of the people of Donegal, I congratulate all those involved in bringing the Agnes Jones Project to such a remarkable conclusion.

I am confident that the documentary-drama and book recounting this pioneering woman's life and work will ensure this unsung heroine of our county finally gains the recognition she deserves. She must now take her rightful place in history as the founder of Irish nursing.

In her vision, compassion and dedication, it is easy to draw parallels between Agnes Jones's mission and that of Mother Teresa of Calcutta. Nurse Jones had, in her own words, come to Liverpool to *'close the eyes of the dying'*. That she achieved so much more in her three short years at the Brownlow Hill workhouse is a tribute to her tenacity and determination to challenge authority. It also explains the respect and affection with which she was regarded among her fellow countrymen and women who had fled poverty and starvation in post-famine Ireland only to abandon their dreams in the Liverpool slums.

May Agnes Jones's life and work be an inspiration to us all.

Mayor Enda Bonner
Donegal County Council

Chapter One

CHILDHOOD

Agnes Elizabeth Jones was born on 10 November 1832 to a military family. Both her parents were Irish. Her father, Joseph, was a native of Ranelagh in County Wicklow, while her mother, Elizabeth Smyth, came from Glendermott in County Derry. The family travelled the world with Joseph's regimental postings. He was a Major in the 12th Regiment of Foot, or infantry, and arrived in Cambridgeshire just days before Agnes was born, prematurely.

Agnes and her younger sister Josephine Mary spent their early years at Fahan House in Donegal until 1837 when Joseph was posted to Mauritius for six years. Their brother Fred was born there, leaving their mother in poor health from which she never fully recovered. Described as delicate and frail, she was often bedridden for long periods and the family was destined to travel extensively throughout Europe in search of a *'climate which might suit her'*. The exact nature of her illness is not recorded, though it appears she suffered with nervous problems, possibly depression, which was also to trouble Agnes in later life.

Joseph's health was also declining and in 1843 he sold his commission and brought the family back to Fahan House, where he lived out his days in retirement. Eleven-year-old Agnes was already starting to record her *'secret life'*, as she termed it, in a series of detailed journals. Surprisingly, for a girl who was an avid reader and who was to become fluent in at least four languages, a succession of governesses found her *'dull'* and *'introspective'*. This may be partly explained by the fact that Agnes had a hearing impairment and suffered from debilitating migraines. She would spend long periods of time, alone, walking along the shores of Lough Swilly, taking in the beautiful views. She was to refer nostalgically to the Donegal coastline's spectacular scenery throughout her life as something which gave her comfort during her virtual incarceration in the urban austerity of Brownlow Hill workhouse.

As a fourteen-year-old, Agnes, who was already filled with evangelical zeal and a determination to help the sick and the poor, recorded her secret ambition to work as a missionary:

> Today, I am fourteen. Quite grown up! Girls of sixteen are getting married. By now, they say, I should know what path my life is taking. I tell no-one, but I still believe my life will be spent caring for the sick. I don't yet know how . . . people tell me I am too stupid, and not conscientious enough in my studies. But it is what I shall do. I know it . . .

Unfortunately, many of her journals are lost to posterity, possibly destroyed after her death.

The sisters were sent to school in Stratford-on-Avon for two years, which seems to have been a positive experience for Agnes.

Then, in March 1850 when she was seventeen, her father's health worsened and he died at Ardmore in Derry, aged fifty-five. It's understood he was being cared for there by his wife's relatives. With her mother an invalid and a boisterous younger brother in Fahan, Agnes and Josephine came home for good. Agnes, who described herself as devastated by her father's death, was now effectively head of the household, nurse, surrogate mother and manager of their declining financial affairs.

Chapter Two

FOLLOWING THE DREAM

Agnes was to spend the next three years caring for her home and family, but never gave up on her belief that she had a vocation. She read extensively about different centres that were providing hands-on nursing care in a Christian setting. In Donegal itself, hardly a week went by when she was not sent for to tend to a sick child, to read and pray with a bedridden invalid, or to comfort the dying.

Most of the local community could not afford a doctor, nor could they pay for their children's education. Agnes drew on examples she had seen in the Dublin area and set up small hedge schools, teaching groups of children basic literacy and numeracy skills. In the summer, she travelled to the west of Ireland to do the same and began fundraising to pay for schoolmasters' salaries.

When she was twenty, an aunt decided to formally complete the girls' education, which had been cut short when their father died, by taking them and their mother on an extended six-month vacation, travelling through France, Germany and Switzerland. This wasn't unusual for young women from their background; Fred, it's understood, stayed at home. Doctors also thought the continental climate might improve their mother's health. They were trying everything.

During that vacation, Agnes persuaded her mother to allow her to spend a week on the German island of Kaisersworth.

Kaisersworth exemplified her ideals of Christian care. A community of weavers there had been faced with starvation when their landlord went bankrupt. They were rescued from their despair by an evangelical preacher, Theodor Fliedner. He turned the whole island into what could best be described as a community-based care organisation and hospital. He had 300 trained staff working at fifteen different centres, setting up orphanages, homes for the aged, lodging houses, schools, and specialist hospitals, where women pharmacists developed new medicines. In mental health care especially, Kaisersworth was a century ahead of its time.

'There are no locked wards, no screaming and crying . . . they have dignity,' Agnes wrote of the mental patients Her week there became a month. She was, in her own words, *'a willing convert and disciple'.*

Chapter Three

TRAINING

The year 1856 was the next turning point for Agnes Jones.

Back in Fahan, Josephine married the local curate, the Reverend Robert Higginbotham, and together they carried out a hands-on pastoral ministry among their parishioners. They also had the duty of caring for the girls' mother, Elizabeth, who was virtually bedridden, and were trying to maintain some control over their younger brother. As with many unconventional sons of the gentry of their time, Fred has virtually disappeared from the family history. We know that by 1859 he was either persuaded (or made) to emigrate to Australia to begin a new life. He returned to London, briefly, in 1867/8, but did not travel on to Ireland, before setting off again, this time for the Friendly Islands, where he intended to start farming. Nothing further was recorded.

Then, totally unexpectedly, in August 2006, Fred's great-grandson, Peter Jones, who lives in New Zealand, contacted the author. Peter Jones began researching his genealogy just three years ago and was excited to discover details of the Agnes project on the Internet. He has kindly supplied the rest of his antecedent's life story – details which have, until now, remained shrouded in mystery.

Fred married late in life; his wife was one of seventeen children of a settler's family. They had seven children. The family finally settled in Tonga, where Peter's grandfather, Hugh, was born. The present-day Jones family in New Zealand are descendants of Hugh and his brother Reg. They have uncovered memorabilia of their celebrated ancestor, including letters Agnes exchanged with her family in Fahan, and with Florence Nightingale. They hope, eventually, to have these permanently housed in a museum.

In European affairs of state, 1856 marked the end of the three-year Crimean War, the conflict between Russia and a coalition of Britain, France, Sardinia and the Ottoman Empire. Politically, it was a major turning point in the history of post-Napoleonic Europe; medically, a catalyst in the development of modern-day nursing.

In military terms, the war had been a blundering, needlessly costly affair, where the commanders of both sides had proved themselves hopelessly inept, squandering life in senseless engagements like the ill-fated Charge of the Light Brigade. Medical services were appalling. More men were to die of disease than on the battlefield. Supply services to both armies were hampered by inefficiency and corruption. Yet the intervention of Florence Nightingale, and the first teams of what were known as the Nightingale Nurses in the field hospitals, effectively reduced the mortality rate from injuries by more than forty per cent, despite the primitive conditions and basic resources.

Even before Florence Nightingale had returned from the Crimea, a public meeting in London had decided to raise a fund to establish a training school – following her methods – for nurses. It was the only public honour she was to accept in her lifetime. For the next few years, her preoccupation was with army sanitary reform, which she considered more urgent. It was 1861 before she first advertised for probationers.

Agnes, who was now back in Kaisersworth, was playing an integral role in running the medical centres there. She was inspired by what she read about Miss Nightingale and began corresponding with her. Agnes wrote to Josephine:

> My prayers are with you as I read of the fever epidemic sweeping through our parish . . . you must both be exhausted working with the sick. I am quite exhausted myself but do not worry mother about it, for I am as happy as the day is long, and the days are never long enough.
>
> I am up at five, make my bed and read until just after six. Then breakfast and prayers, go to the hospital for seven and give the children their medicine; washing and dressing until half past eight. Prepare the children's luncheon, and many need fed, then more washing and after our meal, I take some of the children for a walk till two in the afternoon, then church and more medicines at four. At five, washing and undressing for bed, then supper, and some evenings I am in charge of the whole hospital until half past nine. This is my daily routine and leaves little time for homesickness, though you are always in my thoughts.
>
> Sometimes I work on the male wards, where my duties are varied. I am as likely to be washing dishes or dusting and cleaning as sitting with a dying man . . .
>
> Mother tells me she has heard again from Ellen Raynard at the London Bible Mission and that she would like me to take charge of a dormitory for fifty girls there, which is now under construction. I shall write to her tomorrow when I am less tired but will be cautious in my acceptance, for I feel that my calling is indeed to London, not to a mission but to St Thomas's hospital as a probationer – a Nightingale Nurse. Just seeing

those words in writing excites me. I know mother still feels that full-time nursing is too strenuous and not really for women of our background, and I do not wish to cause her distress . . .

I eagerly await meeting you in London. I shall have with me all my newspaper cuttings I have gathered on this remarkable woman's work in our recent conflict and, most excitingly, the correspondence I have exchanged with her. So, dearest J, you are again part of my secret life.

Your loving sister, a very tired Agnes.

Her time in Germany had passed quickly. Before she left Kaisersworth for good, Agnes had been promoted to take total charge of the children's hospital. Her strong nerve made her ideal for attending at operations such as those for babies' and children's hare lip, which were carried out without any anaesthetic. But she never considered joining the community as a deaconess. These were care sisters whose role was a combination of nurse, childminder, evangelist and Anglican nun.

Agnes Jones returned to London and spent some months working with Ellen Raynard at the London Bible Mission, caring for dormitories of destitute women and girls and visiting the mothers in the slums around Drury Lane. But she had no intention of joining the Bible Women, as they were known. She was on her way to becoming a trained nurse, at last.

Chapter Four

NURSING FOR REAL

Agnes Jones answered Florence Nightingale's historic advertisement in the London *Times* for *Women of good character aged between 25 and 35 years,* and was accepted as one of the first twelve probationers. She was the only Irish woman among the twelve who started training at St Thomas's in September 1862, shortly before her thirtieth birthday. It had been left to Josephine to break the news to their mother, who was still unsure about whether it was a suitable career.

Earlier, Agnes's mentor, Florence Nightingale, had written to her:

> Nursing is an art, and if it is to be made an art, it requires as exclusive a devotion, as hard a preparation as any painter's or sculptor's work . . . for what is having to deal with dead canvas or cold marble compared to having to do with the living body, the temple of God's spirit . . . it is one of the fine arts, I have almost said the finest of the fine arts . . .

Or, as Agnes wrote to her younger sister:

> . . . a far cry from the realm of untrained, ignorant, dirty and sometimes inebriated women our mother fears I would be working among.

During their year's training, the probationers lived in a wing of the hospital, in small, simply furnished rooms. They received free board and lodging, with tea and sugar provided, as well as *'three plain brown dresses and aprons, a certain amount of outer clothing and ten shillings a year'*. Candidates were required to be *'of good appearance, sober, honest, trustworthy, punctual, quiet and orderly, clean and neat'*.

Their intensive training schedule included:

> Number One – the dressing of wounds and application of fomentations, poultices etc in the method of friction to the body and extremities. Attending operations. To be competent in cooking gruel, to understand ventilation, and to manage convalescents.

The correspondence between Agnes and Josephine at this time is heavy with biblical references and a model of correctness, but there seems little doubt that Josephine, who was by now widowed, childless and in poor health herself, was often weighed down under the burden of caring for their mother on an ever-decreasing budget. She was also trying to continue the pastoral work carried out by her husband, which had led to his premature death from fever contracted while ministering to the sick. Agnes was freed from these responsibilities to devote herself totally to her studies.

As Agnes came to the end of her training, the philanthropist and education reformer William Rathbone was becoming increasingly concerned with the way his fellow church members were managing the Liverpool workhouse. Despite his repeated intervention, there was no escaping the fact that *'three senior persons (untrained in nursing) controlled, more or less, a large number of able-bodied pauper assistants, together with a number of scourers (cleaners)'*. This in a workhouse

which could at any one time accommodate up to 1,500 people sleeping eight to a bed.

Many of the workhouse guardians paid lip service to charity, while caring only that the Brownlow Hill workhouse and orphanage operated at a profit. Epidemic after epidemic spread through its inmates: hygiene was appalling; the police patrolled the wards; drunkenness was rife among staff and inmates alike. Among the most tragic figures were the Irish who had fled the aftermath of the Famine aboard an emigrant ship, only to be forced to disembark, ill, penniless and homeless, at the first port of call – Liverpool. An astounding 1.3 million Irish emigrants walked through the dock gates, many to die in unmarked graves. Rathbone took the revolutionary decision to put a woman in charge – a woman who had been trained as a nurse. He sent for Agnes Jones. She answered the call.

Chapter Five

BROWNLOW HILL WORKHOUSE

Agnes Jones took up her post as superintendent of Brownlow Hill in the spring of 1865. At the age of thirty-two, she was effectively in charge of one of England's largest workhouses, with an average population of 1,350, often rising to 1,500. For more than a month, she was to work – unaided – as she waited for more trained nurses to arrive from St Thomas's, where the original probationers were now training more nurses to follow them.

She had an inauspicious beginning when the porter, who did not recognise her, turned her away at the gate. But, once established in her own small room in the workhouse, Agnes began a punishing daily routine, which began at half-past-five in the morning and rarely ended before midnight.

Conditions appalled her. Families were kept apart – husbands from wives, parents from children. The building was filthy. There was a bread shortage and rationing had been introduced. Supplies of food were, all too often, exchanged for alcohol, as inebriation was rife among staff and inmates alike. Agnes writes in her journal of a typical incident in the dining room:

> One unfortunate woman began complaining about her ration and another two attacked her with hairpins

> to try to steal it . . . they nearly scratched her eyes out and they have broken her skin . . . the last time that happened to one of the nurses, she contracted an infection that lasted weeks.

But she was in charge now, and determined to enforce law and order. The police were asked to stop patrolling the wards, unless they were sent for in an emergency. Conditions in the women's wing, in particular, appalled Agnes. Scenes recorded in her journal include:

> A wretched woman was brought in yesterday so in despair that when she eventually gave birth to her infant she slit its throat . . . another baby was found lying in the street almost frozen with its cord still around its neck . . . it was only twelve hours old, but we were able to revive it . . . that is why we are needed . . . nothing is beyond my strength.

Despite opposition from the existing staff, Agnes introduced basic education classes for adults and children. She gave the inmates paper and envelopes and taught them to write home. She set up a library and brought in fresh flowers. Cleanliness and order were established, until fifty wards were fully functional. Menus were overhauled. Bible instruction was optional – but encouraged – provided that the Catholic inmates *'were not acting against their wishes'.* Agnes records that it was a *'popular comfort'.* Within weeks of arriving, she wrote home:

> A hospital is a sad place, but a workhouse . . . it almost seems as if over so many of these beds NO HOPE must be written, with reference to this world. Friendless, hopeless.

Already I have begun the task of reorganising the wards, ready for the arrival of my fellow sisters next month for, as it is, I must go up and down the flight of seventy steps at least fifty times a day.

My day begins at half past five when I unlock the doors for the kitchen women . . . we have prayers an hour later. Then, from seven, I am on the wards to make sure the breakfasts are satisfactory. I am usually on the wards until noon, when I lunch with the other staff. The rest of the afternoon is devoted to the more seriously ill patients. Tea is at four, then I am back on the wards to supervise dressings and I am on and off the ward until the night supervisors arrive at nine. Then prayers again, and a final ward round to ensure all are settled before I return to my own room, where I am now, for paperwork and a little rest.

Our patients come from many backgrounds . . . the French and Italian families have told me they are delighted that I can converse with them in their native language. There are many, many Irish patients who fill entire wards. They are rather amused that unlike them I am not a Catholic. Some of them have asked to attend my prayers, but I must be assured this is entirely of their own volition.

In the afternoon, as I said, I try to devote my time to the more seriously ill patients . . . sitting and talking with them may be all I can do, but it seems to be a comfort. Simple things like bringing them writing paper are very little but they have told me how they welcome this. I am in the process of setting up a small library, too, and I often read to them.

Then, a hurried postscript:

> Lest this sounds like I am complaining, let me tell you that Mr Rathbone described me yesterday as *'the picture of happiness'* and I know that I am completely at home here.

Reforms continued at a rapid pace, despite opposition from the established order who referred wryly to her *'Hibernian rows'* and described her as *'a stiff-necked woman from Ulster with a hot Irish temper'.* Agnes pressed ahead, undeterred and uncompromising. Under her supervision, Brownlow Hill, a supposedly Christian institution, celebrated its first-ever traditional Christmas, with gifts, cakes, a dinner, carol singing, evergreens, and a magic lantern show. Agnes declared it a success, reporting proudly that, despite the extra alcohol ration, *'only two women were sent home for inebriation'.*

Cholera epidemics spread through Liverpool on an almost annual basis, interspersed with typhus and other fevers. Dealing with illness on this scale took its toll on Agnes Jones, physically and mentally. So did the problem of alcohol abuse, which was out of control in urban slums. She wrote in her journal in 1867:

> Sometimes I wonder what sort of place Liverpool is . . . they are discharged cured . . . then they are back three weeks later with delirium tremens, their clothes have not been changed in the meantime . . . many of them have developed sores and ulcers . . . sometimes I fear that this city contains some of the vilest individuals in the country – am I teaching them nothing? Is there no real hope?

By 1 March that year, nevertheless, her progress report for Rathbone was complete, and on the seventh of that month

the vestry presented its own conclusions. Their report could scarcely have been more favourable. Agnes had got her way. From then on, the nursing staff would have total control of how the workhouse, and its funds, was administered.

> I am fighting here for the future of nursing as a whole to ensure it is in the control of those with authority in nursing matters and not those who merely administer the money. That will be my legacy.

So it was to prove.

Her achievements had been threefold: she had made the Liverpool workhouse a model for the rest of the country; she had given the nursing staff administrative and financial control; and she had made the nursing profession respectable.

Chapter Six

TRIBUTES

The strength – physically at least – was no longer there, and Agnes Jones died four days after falling ill with fever, probably cholera, on 19 February 1838. She was thirty-five and had been at the workhouse less than three years – years in which she revolutionised its existence and strengthened the foundations for the future of the nursing profession.

The streets around the workhouse were thronged with mourners as her coffin began its journey to Donegal. Inmates are reported as *'weeping openly, or standing in silent grief'* as the cortège passed. Flowers were strewn along the road in one of the biggest public displays of mourning the city had seen.

Yet responses to her mentor and friend William Rathbone's plans for a memorial were lukewarm, to say the least. He contacted her younger sister. A letter signed by Josephine Jones Higginbotham was sent from Nice, where, she explained, she was staying with her mother in another (ill-fated) attempt to improve her physical and mental health. She wrote that her mother would not even respond to Rathbone's request for suggestions for a memorial, as *'writing was bad for her'*. Josephine asked him, on their behalf, *'not to think of such a thing'*. In a final, sharp comment the letter *'exonerated him from any blame for letting her sister overwork'*. For the family, the subject was closed.

Florence Nightingale was to pay glowing tributes to Agnes in the letters she exchanged with William Rathbone when each was nearing the end of a long life. But, at the time, she was against public recognition for Agnes. She wrote to Rathbone that any memorial *'must be done without asking her leave'*, revealing she preferred to *'let God keep her memory'*. She also suggested that any biography of Agnes should *'be only a sketch'*, scarcely concealing the jealousy which she was reported to feel about her protégée who had enjoyed such popularity among her charges.

Florence Nightingale later wrote a memoir of Agnes, entitled *Una and the Lion,* an allegorical piece depicting Una, or Agnes, as the founder of workhouse nursing taking on the lion of bureaucracy and authority; it neglected to mention Una's real name. Josephine's recollections of her sister, also published later in life, refer to *Una and her Paupers.*

Undeterred, Rathbone pressed ahead, commissioning the respected Roman sculptor Peter Tenerari to carve a memorial statue. He paid for it himself – just as he had paid for the workhouse's first three years of professional nursing. Originally erected in the workhouse itself, the imposing angel-topped plinth was moved first to Liverpool's Walton Hospital, and then to the oratory opposite the Anglican cathedral. Its inscription reads: *In Service, She Lost Her Life.*

The vestry members Agnes had converted to her philosophy of care passed a resolution on their:

> . . . grateful sense of the devoted self-sacrificing and faithful service of the late Miss Jones as Lady Superintendent of Nurses in the Liverpool workhouse hospital . . . they can have little hope of ever again finding one who will combine such a religious sense of duty with such powers of influencing, under much difficulty, those over whom she was placed.

Best of all they remained committed, morally and financially, to continuing her work and the probationers' training scheme.

Agnes Jones remains a legendary figure, even a folk heroine, in the history of Liverpool to this day.

Her memorial tablet in St Mura's Church of Ireland Church in Fahan, where she had worshipped, bears an inscription by the Jones family's friend, Bishop William Alexander of Derry and Raphoe. It remembers Agnes as *'a gentle worker for the gentle Lord'.*

Agnes herself is buried in the old graveyard a few hundred yards away, alongside her father. Her inscription says, rather cryptically:

> She hath done what she could, for the love of Christ constrained her.

Her brother-in-law, the Reverend Robert Higginbotham, whose death was a precursor of her own, lies nearby. Agnes Jones's simple grave is tended by well-wishers.

Florence Nightingale Letter

Below is the transcript of a recently discovered letter from Florence Nightingale to Agnes's mother and sister, Elizabeth Jones and Josephine Jones Higginbotham, following Agnes's death. Reproduced courtesy of Fred Jones's descendant, Peter Jones from New Zealand, who has the original.

35 South Street
Park Lane
London W
22 February 1868

I trust, dear Madam, that you will not think of me as a stranger intermeddling with your grief. You would not, if you knew what dear Agnes was to me – is to me. (I do not like to say *my* dear friend but God's dear friend, Agnes.)

I have never known any like her and never shall again. She had the humility of a child and the power, quietness and activity of a General. She never seemed to know that she was doing anything great. And she lived and died like the Saints and Martyrs. She had a greater power of carrying her followers with her than any woman.

I can't think how I ever could be unhappy, while she was there, doing God's work so gallantly at Liverpool.

And now she is gone.

We know that with her it is "well". But for us, it is terrible. What we are to do without her, I cannot think. How to supply her place – to fill it will be forever impossible.

I want to tell you that our darling was very happy during the year of her Liverpool life – though scarcely any one knows what she went through but God. But I believe they were the happiest years of her life. She was so filled with the thought of doing her "Father's business". And she did it, indeed.

I cannot think how people can look on the power of business as a secondary thing. Agnes could do and did more of her Father's Business in six hours than most women do in six months. She was very happy.

I was afraid you might think that she had troubles she did not tell you of, for fear of making you uneasy. But I believe she told me all her cares and anxieties – not in the way of confidences (she was too wise for that) but that we might consult together as to what was to be done. During the last three years she kept up with me a close correspondence, all on the subjects of her business. That business I know no-one but herself who could have done. And now, just when she had overcome all difficulties and brought the whole arrangements into something like order, God has taken her away from us.

We have to let her kill herself with hard work. But it was not carelessly or for lack of thought. To us this is a never-to-be-forgotten misery. An insupportable grief. But if she could speak, she would say, it is all-well.

I will not make a noise in the great silence of your grief, dear Madam, by telling you the great efforts we all made this last year, Mr Rathbone and I and others, to persuade her to go away for a few weeks (she was under a promise to come to me), to have an assistant, and other things. So did Mrs Wardroper.

She thought that she could not till all the new arrangements were made. And perhaps she was right. At least may we all believe that this great sacrifice may not have been in vain. I do not believe it will. I believe that every workhouse in the Kingdom will feel the effects for good.

But – our darling is gone.

All her nurses would have died for her. One of them wrote, when danger first appeared, "Oh, this is agony." I had a note from one of the dried up old officials, of the Poor Law Board here, acknowledging her great services and deploring her premature loss. Well they may, for they never will have any one like her in their workhouses. I had the miserable comfort of hearing another day that hers was one of the most valuable lives in England.

And so it was.

I return again and again to the thought that she had a very happy life – and a death to be envied. Again and again during her Liverpool life she thanked me for having persuaded her to take Mr Rathbone's work. She said she had never regretted it for one moment. She reminded me (of what I had myself forgotten) that I had persuaded her by telling her a few simple words Sir John Lawrence (the India Viceroy) had once said to me.

Do you know that she wrote to me scarcely more than a fortnight before she was taken from us, telling me of her illness, and bidding me "not to be anxious".

It is not for her, that we must grieve, but for ourselves and our poor. God's poor, rather. And He will take care of them.

I would not have you suppose that I think her work unfinished. But we must all live and work that it may not go back.

You have perhaps heard that Mrs Smyth, a relative, has been so very good as to say that she would stay on for a little while. That is the best for the nurses that they should be under one who mourns their "dear lady" as they do.

You will perhaps think that the words of comfort run too glibly and that I do not know what a mother's grief is. But you would not if you knew what I have lost in her. It seemed so impossible that I should survive her. She was my darling. And she was so much better than I. Hers was the only branch of the work that I could feel quite sure was all done unto God. She did it so much better than I could have done it. Without the thought of her, it is weary work. And I have to encourage others.

I feel so very much too for her sister. May God comfort you and her. For Man cannot. I knew from Agnes herself how deep her love and devotion for her Mother and Sister were.

She with them – all in one – one in God – the closer and the tenderer, I am sure, for her pursuing a separate work for God, with the full approval and sympathy of her Mother and Sister. Next to her dependence upon God, I believe the consciousness of this approval was her strongest support. It is very seldom given by a Mother and Sister in this world.

Ever yours in sorrow and in sympathy,

Florence Nightingale.

Agnes Stage Play Extracts

These extracts are taken from the stage play *Agnes*, which was performed by the Derry-based writing and performance group Handful Productions at The Playhouse, Artillery Street, Derry, in November/December 2004.

The play draws heavily on Agnes Jones's Journal and her letters to her sister, Josephine. In this scene, Agnes is writing her Journal entry for 10 November 1842 – her fourteenth birthday.

When I look back on the past year, I see nothing but sin, depravity and unhappiness. This morning, I made many good resolutions; I fear too much my own strength for in the course of the day, I broke them all. But I still believe that my life will be spent in caring for the sick. I do not yet know how.

Looks up and speaks.

'But it is what I shall do. I know it.'

Writes again.

One thing I do know is that we shall not travel again as a family. Father's health is also failing – he has resigned his commission so there will be no more army postings abroad. Governesses still come and go, but he talks of sending Josie and myself to school in England when she is a little older. Perhaps the age I am today.

Maybe there I may learn about nursing!

Writes again.

Mother remains in poor health, and Fred is a handful of mischief. Sometimes I think he is getting out of control. I do not know what the future holds, but Mother says we must trust in God. Last week, as a surprise, she had a phrenologist who was visiting the neighbourhood call with us. After he had examined my head and all its bumps, he told me to '*take care, little lady*' as he said my strong will may lead me into great faults. Mother was rather upset at this, but he reassured her that love of my parents and my faith would keep me safe. They laughed anyway, for to them I have neither strong will nor desires. As the years pass, I keep them hidden.

Pats the book and speaks.

'Except from you, my Journal. You keep my secrets.'

The stage play deals with the tireless efforts made by the philanthropist William Rathbone to improve conditions in the Brownlow Hill workhouse in Liverpool. He was supported in his work by figures like Louisa Twining. The daughter of a wealthy business family, Twining was one of the first prison and workhouse visitors who campaigned for drastic reform of the management system.

This scene is set in 1865 in Greenbanks, the Rathbone family home in Liverpool, which now forms part of the University of Liverpool campus. The future MP also contributed greatly to education reform and a University Chair is named after him.

William Rathbone sits at his desk, papers before him. Enter Louisa Twining.

RATHBONE: Louisa! So good of you to come. You have your reports with you?

She places them on the table.

RATHBONE: You look weary.

LOUISA: Dispirited, more likely. William, the officers of the Workhouse Visiting Society are mostly good Christian men and women, but it is impossible at times to make them aware of the hopelessness of the situation. Three more of our guardians have resigned this week. I have the letters here.

RATHBONE: Did they tell you why?

LOUISA: In so many words. Worn down by our apparent inability to make any measurable improvement. There were forty more admissions this week; and the place is already overcrowded beyond belief, but how can we turn people away? Here is a former guardian, who says he is '. . . *dispirited by the ignorance and vulgarity of fellow church members who seem to believe we are pandering to the idle and depraved*'. If only they were there to see what I see.

She sits down.

William, the new Master is a totally unfit person He is untrained – he was formerly a porter at the gate. He is disliked – the complaints are universal – yet here I am, presented with a report from the Society that he is '*economical*'.

RATHBONE: Always the economics taking precedence.

LOUISA: Yes, William, and not the inmates. Tell that to your fellow vestrymen. Yesterday I had to wait for more than an hour, with a large crowd of others, to get a ticket for entry. Society member or not, no-one would listen. I am then told by the nurse who met me – and who was seventy if she was a day, bloated and stupid – that visits to the sick are now to be restricted to one hour a week, because they are, she says, '*too busy*'. One poor woman I saw says her sheets have not been changed for six weeks; another man says he has seen the matron once in his four months there and his bed linen, too, was filthy. The chaplain is remarked on for his absence. Yet I am told that the master (*pulls out the report*) '. . . *keeps order and is economical*'. I shall resign.

RATHBONE: Louisa . . .

LOUISA: I shall, William, unless the vestry do something. Now.

RATHBONE: And that, my dear Louisa, is why I sent for you so urgently. At last night's meeting they finally agreed to introduce trained Nightingale nurses to the infirmary beside the work-house. A small beginning, but a beginning no less. And I have been entrusted to recruit twelve women.

LOUISA: Twelve nurses. For twelve hundred inmates!

RATHBONE: Louisa, we have to start somewhere.

LOUISA: Oh, I agree. It's just so frustrating. What do you think changed their minds? I have been visiting weekly, or twice weekly, and making my reports for some five years now and they never take heed.

RATHBONE: This private report I requested from our friend and correspondent Miss Nightingale can only have helped (*hands it to her*). She likens the conditions to the makeshift field hospitals in the Crimea.

LOUISA: *(reads)* Immorality was universal; filth was universal; the patients wore the same shirts for seven weeks; bedding was only changed and washed once a month; food was at starvation level; spirits entered the infirmary freely.

RATHBONE: How could men of the church live with that indictment? Twelve nurses to start with, and then, I am confident, more to follow. I would hope to open our own training school here, under her supervision. Miss Nightingale has agreed that Liverpool will be her pilot scheme to be copied in London and elsewhere.

LOUISA: And the vestry has been persuaded to fund this?

RATHBONE: The vestry has finally been persuaded that it is vital to the stability and improvement of the city itself. That is why I am today writing to an Irish nurse – Agnes Jones – whom Miss Nightingale has recommended to lead the team as lady superintendent and who, she thinks, will be willing to take up the challenge.

LOUISA: But what about the money? She is a professional woman. She must be paid.

RATHBONE: It will be available.

LOUISA: William Rathbone . . .

RATHBONE: It will be made available initially for three years.

LOUISA: It's you, isn't it? From your own pocket.

RATHBONE: Miss Nightingale is lobbying the Prime Minister for government funding. I know it is a big investment, but I have no option. If something is not done I cannot, in all conscience, remain on the committee responsible for these conditions. Look at it; there are three senior staff – untrained in nursing – trying to control a large number of admittedly able-bodied pauper women who, when they are paid, drink their wages as often as not, as do the scourers who then cease scouring! You have seen it first hand yourself. I have here reports of them stealing the patients' food to eat, then selling their own rations. The police are being called in to patrol the wards at night. If I can make some difference by funding these nurses for just three years, I have no option but to try.

LOUISA: So you will write to this Miss Jones?

RATHBONE: You may read the letter before I post it.

Agnes took up the post, leaving her younger sister to work on convincing their mother that she had made the right decision. From her simple room in the workhouse, she wrote detailed letters home describing the demands of her daily routine.

In this last extract, Agnes's legacy is becoming apparent.

NARRATOR: By July 1867 the vestry presented its own conclusions on an earlier progress report by Agnes on her work to date in the workhouse. Their report could scarcely have been more favourable. In less than two years, Agnes Jones had won the hearts and minds of the well-intentioned, philanthropist and cynic alike, though at great cost to her own health. While her contemporaries shied away from any reports, which could have been perceived as unsympathetic, it's clear that she suffered bouts of severe depression. There are references to her being '*spiritually and physically overtaxed in every way*' and having '*an oversensitive conscience and morbid self condemnation*'.

Greenbanks. Rathbone and Agnes sit at the desk.

RATHBONE: So there it is – the vestry report. You must be satisfied, at least. Your trained nurses, the whole ethos has been validated beyond doubt.

AGNES: And yourself, William? Are you pleased? At least it justifies your own personal investment.

RATHBONE: That never needed justifying, but it is a relief to have it confirmed in writing that from now on the vestry will undertake all financial responsibilities for nursing – and on a permanent basis – and that training can continue on the wards. Agnes, it is a tremendous achievement. Fifty fully-staffed wards in operation.

AGNES: And we can now cater for some three hundred residents above the projected maximum with some degree of comfort. We are not turning away so many who may be in need. But there is still a great deal to be done in the next few weeks.

She produces some papers.

Have you time to consider these? Look, this is a series of formal meetings I have planned with the matron, the storekeepers, and the Clerk of Works. We need to explain the size of sheets we need and the amount, the cut of shirts, bedding requirements and repairs. And there are these changes in the kitchen arrangements to ensure it runs more efficiently. We need to order tables and chairs for the dining area, and forms for the wards. Oh, and here I have plans for Christmas . . .

RATHBONE: Agnes, it's March. It's not even Easter yet!

AGNES: But I must plan. Last year was such a success, with the evergreens decorating the wards, and the tree. The gifts of fruit and money for the patients that you and Emily so generously provided. There were the cakes the kitchen produced, and the nurses' dinner we saved up for, and the magic lantern show. It was very popular, you know. Privately, I was worried it would be spoiled by drunkenness brought on by the extra alcohol rations, but look at the report book.

Opens it.

No fighting. And only two women sent home for inebriation. Even the sick nursing mothers were well behaved, and you know their record. I put it down to the magic lantern show, you know. It was quite excellent.

RATHBONE: *(laughs)* Your innocence is frightening at times. I'd say it was to be put down to excellent supervision, not a few pictures. *(Serious again.)* Remember, there may yet be many struggles ahead with Mr Carr, the governor. He has not taken kindly to Miss Nightingale's ruling that he must have no interference whatsoever in the training of the probationers, and now that has the vestry's backing, you have quite a position of power over him.

AGNES: I am not so innocent, William, and any complaints I have will be put in writing for the select committee, as they have been this past two years. I am well aware Miss Nightingale says she had not received so many submissions of complaint about management in peace time. You and I know Mr Carr wants nothing better than to return to the crude system of initiating pauper assistants with little or no training, and less standards, and to insist it is cheaper.

RATHBONE: *(wryly)* The vestry report does mention in detail his complaints of what he calls '*Hibernian rows*'.

AGNES: And I have heard his description of me as '*a stiff-necked Presbyterian Irishwoman from Ulster with a hot Irish temper*', which I am not. He has criticised my evangelical faith on one hand and yet the same man was reluctant to accept the training of Protestant and Catholic nurses side by side. Where is the logic in that? I am fighting here for the future of nursing as a whole to ensure it is in the control of those with authority in nursing matters and not those who merely administer the money.

Closes books.

AGNES: That will be my legacy.

Taken from the Agnes *stage play. Leona McCreadie as Nurse Gilpin and Felicity McCall as Agnes Jones. Nurse Gilpin is trying in vain to persuade Agnes, who is already gravely ill, to take more rest.*

Agnes Screenplay Extracts

The following are some extracts from the screenplay of the film *Agnes,* which is a joint production between the community and private sectors ie Greater Shantallow Community Arts and Ambient Light Productions, and grant aided by the Northern Ireland Film and Television Commission.

The opening lines of the script made full use of some of Inishowen's most beautiful scenery for the narrator, played by celebrated Irish actor Dan Gordon.

NARRATOR DAY FAHAN

The Donegal village of Fahan, on the shore of Lough Swilly, the lake of a Thousand Eyes, nestling at the foot of Gollan Hill. Traditionally, it was a small, rural community earning its living from fishing and hill farming. Now its expansion comes from its development as a tourist spot with holiday homes and a marina built to international standards. It's also become part of the commuter belt for the city of Derry, which is just eight miles away.

Fahan's monastic roots date back to the sixth century when the abbot Mura, who was one of St Columba's followers, founded his monastery here. The ruins of his church and cross remain. The local patron saint has lent his name to churches, schools and generations of children.

One of the area's most illustrious daughters was to write with great eloquence of the solace she found in its countryside and shore: '. . . *the bank of wild roses on the sand hills above the strand . . . the sunset seen from Buncrana . . . then the full moon in all its grandeur, sailing over the sky and then disappearing behind a cloud, silvering its outline. All these, one after the other, came with a force that seemed to speak peace'.*

NARRATOR PIECE TO CAMERA AT GRAVE

This overgrown graveyard surrounding the ruins of the old St Mura's Parish Church may seem an unprepossessing final resting place for the author of these words. The nursing pioneer Agnes Jones spent her adolescence in the village and went on, during her short life, to revolutionise the whole ethos of workhouse care.

It was to this family plot that her remains were brought from Liverpool where she died, aged just thirty-five, of typhus contracted at the Brownlow Hill workhouse where she lived and ministered among the poor. Many of them were famine emigrants from here who had left Derry quay for a new life in America, only to find their escape to the New World abandoned in the squalor of the Merseyside slums.

By the time Agnes was laid to rest alongside her father, she had transformed the workhouses from places where she had come, in her own words, to *'close the eyes of the dying'*, to havens of hygiene, medical care, education and spiritual instruction. No wonder then that in her adoptive city she is commemorated in both the Catholic and Anglican cathedrals as well as the main hospital as *'an angel who walked among us with a gifted touch'*.

Yet here she lies, largely forgotten. We can only speculate why.

NARRATOR VOICEOVER ARCHIVE PIX

This is a closely-knit community where the same people have farmed the land for generations. The Joneses, as a military family, used to following her father Joseph's regiment around the world, were never fully integrated.

Agnes and her siblings died childless, leaving no-one in the immediate area to keep alive her memory.

And, as events will show, both her relatives and her mentor Florence Nightingale were reluctant to mark her life and work. But that is in the future. It's in Fahan House nearby that her story really begins

HEDGE SCHOOL SCENE

The screenplay included recreations of scenes and events typical of Agnes's own experiences recorded in her Journal, which would not have been feasible on stage. Some of these drafts were eventually cut back for broadcast reasons.

The hedge school scene which follows was filmed outdoors. Agnes is sitting round a small table in the corner of a room in a private house. A group of about a dozen small children, all in well-worn clothing but concentrating intently, are sharing a few slates and chalks.

AGNES: Very good, class! Now, give the chalk to the person sitting on your right; yes, that's it; and it's their turn to copy the letters. Then you can go outside to run about while your older brothers and sisters do their sums with me.

Much scuffling, writing etc.

BOY: Do you think we will ever have a proper school, Miss Jones?

GIRL: This *is* a proper school.

BOY: (*embarrassed*) I meant, with a big classroom of its own.

AGNES: Schools cost money, Peter. What I am doing when I'm not busy teaching you is trying to get the authorities to pay a schoolmaster's wages – that would be a start.

GIRL 2: Could you not stay with us, Miss Jones? I love your stories.

AGNES: Only for a little longer. Then I am moving on to teach some other little boys and girls in Connemara. Does anyone know where that is?

Hands go up as they look at a map of Ireland.

COTTAGE FIRE SCENE

Extracts from her writings chronicle almost daily visits among the poor of the parish in Fahan, where medical facilities were as costly as they were rare.

This scene is based on a disaster which happened near Fahan when Agnes was in her late teens. Again, the final film version had to be edited down because of the required duration.

The father and mother are sitting on a wooden settle with a little girl on the father's lap. She is loosely wrapped in a wet sheet and whimpering. The father has his arm round his wife's shoulders. She is sobbing uncontrollably. The other children are looking on, crying or whispering among themselves. There are the remains of a fire in the grate and a bucket of water lying spilled on the floor. An older boy comes in.

BOY: James is away to fetch Miss Jones now. He said he should have her up here not long after I'm back. He kept asking me how it happened and I kept telling him to hurry. How is she?

FATHER: She's nearly cried herself asleep, thank God. (*To younger ones*) Stay back from your sister now. Can't you see she's suffering?

OLDER GIRL: What can we do for her?

FATHER: We'll just have to wait. And pray. If anyone knows what to do it'll be Miss Jones.

MOTHER: Could we not get the doctor?

FATHER: From Buncrana? By the time we'd find him ... and how would we pay him? Miss Jones is as good as any doctor.

MOTHER: What if she's not at home? What will we do?

FATHER: She'll not be far away. She and her sister are never far from their mother these days. Sure only last week she sat with Teresa's mother for two nights when she was dying (*breaks off awkwardly*). They say Mrs Jones is very failed again. If I'd been here ...

BOY: (*to father*) Don't be taking it out on them. They're only little. It's not their fault, Da. She always complains of the cold and stands right in at the fire. You couldn't watch her.

OLDER GIRL: It wasn't our fault, Da. There was nothing we could do.

YOUNGER GIRL: She said she was cold. She leant too close over the fire to warm herself and her dress just went up in flames.

OLDER GIRL: What can we do?

FATHER: Just keep saying your prayers, Miss Jones won't be long.

BOY: (*whispers*) What do you think?

FATHER: (*shakes his head*) She's bad, very bad . . .

Enter Agnes, knocking, followed by James, the neighbour who went to fetch her in his horse and cart.

AGNES: May I come in? James told me what had happened. The poor little girl (*goes over*). May I?

They watch as she peels back the sheet.

MOTHER: (*screams*) Oh My God, the skin's burned off her!

Child starts to cry too. Father and Agnes exchange glances.

AGNES: That's the water. It has caused the skin to peel away. But you did what you thought was best.

OLDER GIRL: Daddy was putting the fire out.

AGNES: I know, I know. It's all right. Now fetch me some flour. And a clean sheet. It must be clean, mind you, otherwise we risk an infection.

The girl does so.

AGNES: I'll sprinkle a little bit of flour on the burns to protect the skin. It might help to ease the pain as well. Then we'll wrap her in this cloth to keep the air off the rawness. And we must put her down to sleep, she's exhausted with the shock and the pain.

YOUNGER GIRL: Is she going to die?

BOY: Shush! No, she's not (*looks at father*).

AGNES: Only God knows that. We will do what we can (*looks at parents*). I only wish I could do more.

BREAD FIGHT SCENE KITCHEN

The documentary-drama also includes scenes recreated from Agnes Jones's descriptions of everyday life in the workhouse, including one of her dispiriting setbacks when she was forced to abandon a second training scheme aimed at the female pauper assistants. They had been popular with the previous management because they were readily available and easily paid, if not often clean, sober or educated. A fever epidemic, combined with a bread shortage in 1867, led to reports of assistants spending their wages on alcohol then stealing the patients' bread supplies. Physical fighting over food was also commonplace

Supervisors are seen hiding bread. One grabs another's bundle, they start to fight, scratching, hair pulling, as a young nurse tries to keep them apart.

WOMAN 1: Give that here, you thieving bitch, that's mine. I got a market for that!

WOMAN 2: Lay off, it's mine! You bitch! Get off me, you bloody drunk!

They scrabble on the floor as a porter comes in and drags them apart.

PORTER: Problems, nurse?

Laughs at her. Grabs the two women and drags them to the door.

PORTER: Out, you two and don't come back till you're sober!

WOMAN 1: Give us me bread!

PORTER: To sell for drink? Earn your money the way you used to, you thieving baggage!

He drags them out and returns shortly after as the nurse is cleaning up.

PORTER: Filth, nurse. Fishwives, the pair of them. One's as bad as the other. And to think your Miss Jones was wanting to train them (*snorts*). There's only one thing they're good for, and it's not nursing. (*He takes the bread from the nurse.*) Now, if you don't mind, I can be using that myself – or are you going to tell your Miss Jones on me?

Walks off, whistling.

But there were times, too, however brief, when Agnes was able to share in the atmosphere she had striven to create. The film includes a scene of the first ever Christmas celebrations held in that purportedly most Christian of institutions, the Parish workhouse. A child sings a carol written just a short time earlier by Agnes's close friend from Ireland, the Bishop of Derry's wife, Cecil Frances Alexander. The pure tones of *Once in Royal David's City* mark the season for close on two thousand souls for whom it would otherwise have passed like any other day in the slums of Liverpool.

Bibliography

All the quotations are taken directly from Agnes Jones's own letters and those of her family, friends and colleagues. Unfortunately, as with so many Victorians, her own diaries have been lost to posterity and little written contemporary evidence remains of her life.

For those who would like to read more about her life, sources to track down include:

A Gifted Touch by James and John Ross.

William Rathbone's collected letters.

Memorials of Agnes Jones by her Sister, by Josephine Jones Higginbotham, a version of which is also published as *Una and her Paupers.*

Una and her Paupers can be obtained from Diggory Press www.diggorypress.com

Agnes Film Images

These images are taken from the filming of *Agnes* in July 2006, directed by Eoin Coffey. They show Bronagh Gallagher in the title role and Dan Gordon as the narrator. Also included are Aoife Madden and Damien Hasson as the Higginbothams, and Seamus Ball as the workhouse porter. The locations include the Ulster American Folk Park in Omagh; Derry locations such as the Workhouse Museum, St Columb's Cathedral, Prehen House and the former Ebrington Barracks; and Inch House in County Donegal.

Location photography: Paola Bernardelli. Images courtesy of Ambient Light Productions.

Additional photography: Oliver Green. Images courtesy of Greater Shantallow Community Arts.

SONY
HDV

J.DEVLIN

SINNER
FEAR HIM

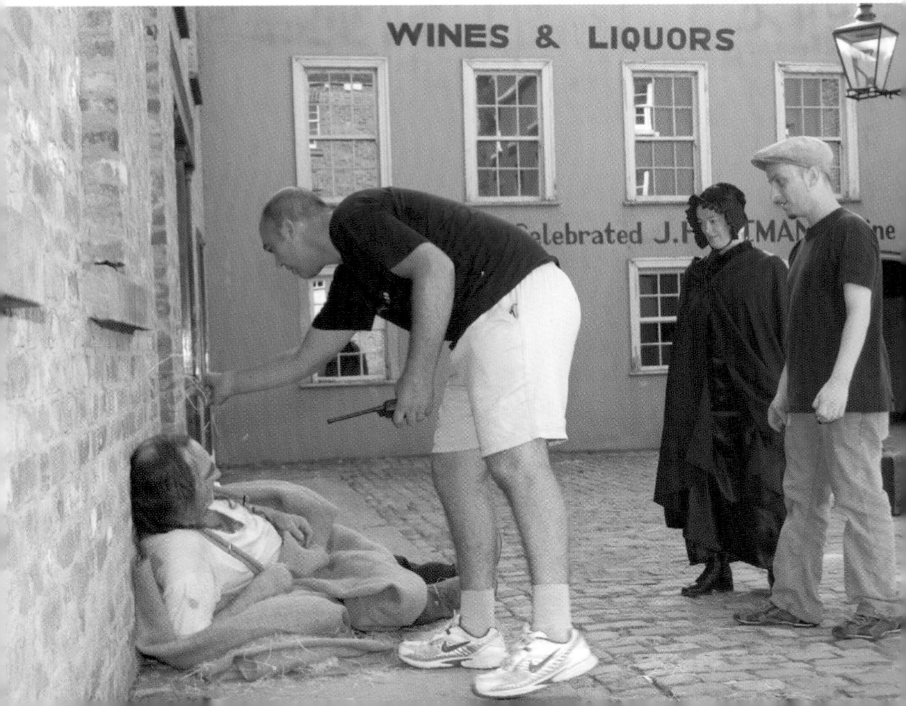

WINES & LIQUORS
Celebrated

Above: Director Eoin Coffey, producer Tony Doherty and the Agnes *film production crew.*
Below: Members of the cast of the stage play Agnes *with director Bernie Mahon (2nd left) visit Agnes Jones's grave at Fahan. (L-R) Aine Fitzpatrick (young Josie), Leona McCreadie (Kitty/ Nurse Gilpin), Allan Moore (warden), Felicity McCall (Agnes), Aoife Morrow (young Agnes).*